Join Our Team
Achieve a Dream
Knowledge Changes You
You Change the World

GOOD GRADES BECOME GRAND DREAMS

Daily Habits Daily Rewards
Take Control of Your Day, Your Dream & Your Destiny

This book is not an orphan.
If lost, please return to:

Name: _____

School: _____

Grade: _____

For Academic Success in School,
Personal Success at Home,
and Professional Success at Work

SMARTGRADES Class Schedule

Monday	Class	Time	Room	Teacher
1st Class				
2nd Class				
3rd Class				
4th Class				
5th Class				

Tuesday
1st Class				
2nd Class				
3rd Class				
4th Class				
5th Class				

Wednesday
1st Class				
2nd Class				
3rd Class				
4th Class				
5th Class				

Thursday
1st Class				
2nd Class				
3rd Class				
4th Class				
5th Class				

Friday
1st Class				
2nd Class				
3rd Class				
4th Class				
5th Class				

Daily Habits, Daily Rewards

Take Control of Your Day, Your Dream & Your Destiny

What's Inside

- Academic Calendar

- Class Schedule

- Homework Assignment Planner

- Study Schedule Planner

- Setting Priorities

- Time Management

- Self-Esteem Builder

- Energy Planner

- Menu Planner

- Budget and Expense Planner

- After School Activities Planner

- Family Chores Planner

- Journal of True Feelings

- Grade Tracker

- Teacher Contact Information

- Study Buddy Contact Information

- Bedtime Planner

- PHOTON'S 10 Facts of Academic Success

Academic Calendar: August-January

August

Class	What's Due?	Due Date

Back to School: Get Organized, Prepare Study Room, Purchase School Supplies

----

September

October

November

December

January

Academic Calendar: February-June

February Class	What's Due?	Due Date
---------------	---------------	---------------
---------------	---------------	---------------
---------------	---------------	---------------

March

---------------	---------------	---------------
---------------	---------------	---------------
---------------	---------------	---------------

April

---------------	---------------	---------------
---------------	---------------	---------------
---------------	---------------	---------------

May

---------------	---------------	---------------
---------------	---------------	---------------
---------------	---------------	---------------

June

---------------	---------------	---------------
---------------	---------------	---------------
---------------	---------------	---------------

My Homework Assignments

Today's Date:

My Homework: Read Chapter, Write Paper, Solve Problem, Ace Test

1st Assignment
Subject:
Due Date:

2nd Assignment
Subject:
Due Date:

3rd Assignment
Subject:
Due Date:

4th Assignment
Subject:
Due Date:

5th Assignment
Subject:
Due Date:

6th Assignment
Subject:
Due Date:

My Study Schedule

❑ **Study Period 1 (45 Minute Study & 15 Minute Break)**
Subject:
❑ Daily Test Review Notes to Ace Tests
Start Time: _____   Finish Time: _____

❑ **Study Period 2**
Subject:
❑ Daily Test Review Notes to Ace Tests
Start Time: _____   Finish Time: _____

❑ **Study Period 3**
Subject:
❑ Daily Test Review Notes to Ace Tests
Start Time: _____   Finish Time: _____

❑ **Study Period 4**
Subject:
❑ Daily Test Review Notes to Ace Tests
Start Time: _____   Finish Time: _____

❑ **Study Period 5**
Subject:
❑ Daily Test Review Notes to Ace Tests
Start Time: _____   Finish Time: _____

Priority #1
Study for Test!

Priority #2
What's due tomorrow?

Priority #3
Math/Science?

Priority #4
English/History?

Priority #5
What time is dinner?

Priority #6
Write and Review: "My Daily Test Review Notes" to Ace Every Test Everytime!

Priority #7
Socialize with Family & Friends

Priority #8
Get Ready for Tomorrow!

Get Ready for Tomorrow:
❑ Pack Book Bag: Textbooks and Notebooks
❑ Checklist: Keys, School I.D., Wallet, Money, Pens, Pencils
❑ Check Weather (Umbrella?)
❑ Prepare School Clothing
❑ Charge Electronics
❑ Kiss Loved Ones
❑ Brush and Floss Teeth
❑ Set Alarm Clock
❑ **9-11 P.M. Regular Bedtime for Sleep Energy**

My Energy: Mind, Body and Spirit

Today's Positive Thoughts (My Self-Esteem Energy):

Today's Real Food Energy Choices:

Breakfast Energy: _____

Lunch Energy: _____

Dinner Energy: _____

Power Study Snacks: _____

Today's Exercise Energy (Break a Sweat!) : _____

Tonight's Regular Bedtime Energy: _____ P.M.

My Budget: Save, Spend, and Splurge

Total Amount: $ _____

Pay Yourself First: $ _____ My Savings

EXPENSES: NEEDS AND WANTS

Spend(Needs): $ _____

Splurge (Wants): $ _____

Total Expenses: $ _____

My Pocket Money: $ _____

My After School Family Chores

1.

2.

3.

My After School Activities

1.

2.

3.

My Journal of True Feelings

The Best Part of My Day:

The Worst Part of My Day:

❑ Great Day   ❑ Good Day   ❑ Stressful Day

My Homework Assignments

Today's Date:

My Homework: Read Chapter, Write Paper, Solve Problem, Ace Test

1st Assignment
Subject:
Due Date:

_____

2nd Assignment
Subject:
Due Date:

_____

3rd Assignment
Subject:
Due Date:

_____

4th Assignment
Subject:
Due Date:

_____

5th Assignment
Subject:
Due Date:

_____

6th Assignment
Subject:
Due Date:

_____

My Study Schedule

❏ **Study Period 1 (45 Minute Study & 15 Minute Break)**
Subject:
❏ Daily Test Review Notes to Ace Tests
Start Time: _____ Finish Time: _____

❏ **Study Period 2**
Subject:
❏ Daily Test Review Notes to Ace Tests
Start Time: _____ Finish Time: _____

❏ **Study Period 3**
Subject:
❏ Daily Test Review Notes to Ace Tests
Start Time: _____ Finish Time: _____

❏ **Study Period 4**
Subject:
❏ Daily Test Review Notes to Ace Tests
Start Time: _____ Finish Time: _____

❏ **Study Period 5**
Subject:
❏ Daily Test Review Notes to Ace Tests
Start Time: _____ Finish Time: _____

Priority #1
Study for Test!

Priority #2
What's due tomorrow?

Priority #3
Math/Science?

Priority #4
English/History?

Priority #5
What time is dinner?

Priority #6
Write and Review: "My Daily Test Review Notes" to Ace Every Test Everytime!

Priority #7
Socialize with Family & Friends

Priority #8
Get Ready for Tomorrow!

Get Ready for Tomorrow:
❏ Pack Book Bag: Textbooks and Notebooks
❏ Checklist: Keys, School I.D., Wallet, Money, Pens, Pencils
❏ Check Weather (Umbrella?)
❏ Prepare School Clothing
❏ Charge Electronics
❏ Kiss Loved Ones
❏ Brush and Floss Teeth
❏ Set Alarm Clock

❏ **9-11 P.M. Regular Bedtime for Sleep Energy**

My Energy: Mind, Body and Spirit

Today's Positive Thoughts (My Self-Esteem Energy):

Today's Real Food Energy Choices:

Breakfast Energy: _____

Lunch Energy: _____

Dinner Energy: _____

Power Study Snacks: _____

Today's Exercise Energy (Break a Sweat!) : _____

Tonight's Regular Bedtime Energy: _____ P.M.

My Budget: Save, Spend, and Splurge

Total Amount: $ _____

Pay Yourself First: $ _____ My Savings

EXPENSES: NEEDS AND WANTS

Spend(Needs): $ _____

Splurge (Wants): $ _____

Total Expenses: $ _____

My Pocket Money: $ _____

My After School Family Chores

1.

2.

3.

My After School Activities

1.

2.

3.

My Journal of True Feelings

The Best Part of My Day:

The Worst Part of My Day:

❏ Great Day   ❏ Good Day   ❏ Stressful Day

My Homework Assignments

Today's Date:

My Homework: Read Chapter, Write Paper, Solve Problem, Ace Test

1st Assignment
Subject:
Due Date:

2nd Assignment
Subject:
Due Date:

3rd Assignment
Subject:
Due Date:

4th Assignment
Subject:
Due Date:

5th Assignment
Subject:
Due Date:

6th Assignment
Subject:
Due Date:

My Study Schedule

❑ **Study Period 1 (45 Minute Study & 15 Minute Break)**
Subject:
❑ Daily Test Review Notes to Ace Tests
Start Time: _____ Finish Time: _____

❑ **Study Period 2**
Subject:
❑ Daily Test Review Notes to Ace Tests
Start Time: _____ Finish Time: _____

❑ **Study Period 3**
Subject:
❑ Daily Test Review Notes to Ace Tests
Start Time: _____ Finish Time: _____

❑ **Study Period 4**
Subject:
❑ Daily Test Review Notes to Ace Tests
Start Time: _____ Finish Time: _____

❑ **Study Period 5**
Subject:
❑ Daily Test Review Notes to Ace Tests
Start Time: _____ Finish Time: _____

Priority #1
Study for Test!

Priority #2
What's due tomorrow?

Priority #3
Math/Science?

Priority #4
English/History?

Priority #5
What time is dinner?

Priority #6
Write and Review: "My Daily Test Review Notes" to Ace Every Test Everytime!

Priority #7
Socialize with Family & Friends

Priority #8
Get Ready for Tomorrow!

Get Ready for Tomorrow:
❑ Pack Book Bag: Textbooks and Notebooks
❑ Checklist: Keys, School I.D., Wallet, Money, Pens, Pencils
❑ Check Weather (Umbrella?)
❑ Prepare School Clothing
❑ Charge Electronics
❑ Kiss Loved Ones
❑ Brush and Floss Teeth
❑ Set Alarm Clock

❑ **9–11 P.M. Regular Bedtime for Sleep Energy**

My Energy: Mind, Body and Spirit

Today's Positive Thoughts (My Self-Esteem Energy):

Today's Real Food Energy Choices:

Breakfast Energy: _____

Lunch Energy: _____

Dinner Energy: _____

Power Study Snacks: _____

Today's Exercise Energy (Break a Sweat!) : _____

Tonight's Regular Bedtime Energy: _____ P.M.

My Budget: Save, Spend, and Splurge

Total Amount: $ _____

Pay Yourself First: $ _____ My Savings

EXPENSES: NEEDS AND WANTS

Spend(Needs): $ _____

Splurge (Wants): $ _____

Total Expenses: $ _____

My Pocket Money: $ _____

My After School Family Chores

1.

2.

3.

My After School Activities

1.

2.

3.

My Journal of True Feelings

The Best Part of My Day:

The Worst Part of My Day:

❏ Great Day   ❏ Good Day   ❏ Stressful Day

My Homework Assignments

Today's Date:

My Homework: Read Chapter, Write Paper, Solve Problem, Ace Test

1st Assignment
Subject:
Due Date:

2nd Assignment
Subject:
Due Date:

3rd Assignment
Subject:
Due Date:

4th Assignment
Subject:
Due Date:

5th Assignment
Subject:
Due Date:

6th Assignment
Subject:
Due Date:

My Study Schedule

❏ **Study Period 1 (45 Minute Study & 15 Minute Break)**
Subject:
❏ Daily Test Review Notes to Ace Tests
Start Time: _____ Finish Time: _____

❏ **Study Period 2**
Subject:
❏ Daily Test Review Notes to Ace Tests
Start Time: _____ Finish Time: _____

❏ **Study Period 3**
Subject:
❏ Daily Test Review Notes to Ace Tests
Start Time: _____ Finish Time: _____

❏ **Study Period 4**
Subject:
❏ Daily Test Review Notes to Ace Tests
Start Time: _____ Finish Time: _____

❏ **Study Period 5**
Subject:
❏ Daily Test Review Notes to Ace Tests
Start Time: _____ Finish Time: _____

Priority #1
Study for Test!

Priority #2
What's due tomorrow?

Priority #3
Math/Science?

Priority #4
English/History?

Priority #5
What time is dinner?

Priority #6
Write and Review: "My Daily Test Review Notes" to Ace Every Test Everytime!

Priority #7
Socialize with Family & Friends

Priority #8
Get Ready for Tomorrow!

Get Ready for Tomorrow:
❏ Pack Book Bag: Textbooks and Notebooks
❏ Checklist: Keys, School I.D., Wallet, Money, Pens, Pencils
❏ Check Weather (Umbrella?)
❏ Prepare School Clothing
❏ Charge Electronics
❏ Kiss Loved Ones
❏ Brush and Floss Teeth
❏ Set Alarm Clock

❏ **9-11 P.M. Regular Bedtime for Sleep Energy**

My Energy: Mind, Body and Spirit

Today's Positive Thoughts (My Self-Esteem Energy):

Today's Real Food Energy Choices:

Breakfast Energy: _____

Lunch Energy: _____

Dinner Energy: _____

Power Study Snacks: _____

Today's Exercise Energy (Break a Sweat!) : _____

Tonight's Regular Bedtime Energy: _____ P.M.

My Budget: Save, Spend, and Splurge

Total Amount: $ _____

Pay Yourself First: $ _____ My Savings

EXPENSES: NEEDS AND WANTS

Spend(Needs): $ _____

Splurge (Wants): $ _____

Total Expenses: $ _____

My Pocket Money: $ _____

My After School Family Chores

1.

2.

3.

My After School Activities

1.

2.

3.

My Journal of True Feelings

The Best Part of My Day:

The Worst Part of My Day:

❑ Great Day   ❑ Good Day   ❑ Stressful Day

My Homework Assignments

Today's Date:

My Homework: Read Chapter, Write Paper, Solve Problem, Ace Test

1st Assignment
Subject:
Due Date:

2nd Assignment
Subject:
Due Date:

3rd Assignment
Subject:
Due Date:

4th Assignment
Subject:
Due Date:

5th Assignment
Subject:
Due Date:

6th Assignment
Subject:
Due Date:

My Study Schedule

❑ **Study Period 1 (45 Minute Study & 15 Minute Break)**
Subject:
❑ Daily Test Review Notes to Ace Tests
Start Time: _____ Finish Time: _____

❑ **Study Period 2**
Subject:
❑ Daily Test Review Notes to Ace Tests
Start Time: _____ Finish Time: _____

❑ **Study Period 3**
Subject:
❑ Daily Test Review Notes to Ace Tests
Start Time: _____ Finish Time: _____

❑ **Study Period 4**
Subject:
❑ Daily Test Review Notes to Ace Tests
Start Time: _____ Finish Time: _____

❑ **Study Period 5**
Subject:
❑ Daily Test Review Notes to Ace Tests
Start Time: _____ Finish Time: _____

Priority #1
Study for Test!

Priority #2
What's due tomorrow?

Priority #3
Math/Science?

Priority #4
English/History?

Priority #5
What time is dinner?

Priority #6
Write and Review: "My Daily Test Review Notes" to Ace Every Test Everytime!

Priority #7
Socialize with Family & Friends

Priority #8
Get Ready for Tomorrow!

Get Ready for Tomorrow:
❑ Pack Book Bag: Textbooks and Notebooks
❑ Checklist: Keys, School I.D., Wallet, Money, Pens, Pencils
❑ Check Weather (Umbrella?)
❑ Prepare School Clothing
❑ Charge Electronics
❑ Kiss Loved Ones
❑ Brush and Floss Teeth
❑ Set Alarm Clock

❑ **9-11 P.M. Regular Bedtime for Sleep Energy**

My Energy: Mind, Body and Spirit

Today's Positive Thoughts (My Self-Esteem Energy):

Today's Real Food Energy Choices:

Breakfast Energy: _____

Lunch Energy: _____

Dinner Energy: _____

Power Study Snacks: _____

Today's Exercise Energy (Break a Sweat!) : _____

Tonight's Regular Bedtime Energy: _____ P.M.

My Budget: Save, Spend, and Splurge

Total Amount: $ _____

Pay Yourself First: $ _____ My Savings

EXPENSES: NEEDS AND WANTS

Spend(Needs): $ _____

Splurge (Wants): $ _____

Total Expenses: $ _____

My Pocket Money: $ _____

My After School Family Chores

1.

2.

3.

My After School Activities

1.

2.

3.

My Journal of True Feelings

The Best Part of My Day:

The Worst Part of My Day:

❏ Great Day   ❏ Good Day   ❏ Stressful Day

My Homework Assignments

Today's Date:

My Homework: Read Chapter, Write Paper, Solve Problem, Ace Test

1st Assignment
Subject:
Due Date:

2nd Assignment
Subject:
Due Date:

3rd Assignment
Subject:
Due Date:

4th Assignment
Subject:
Due Date:

5th Assignment
Subject:
Due Date:

6th Assignment
Subject:
Due Date:

My Study Schedule

❑ **Study Period 1 (45 Minute Study & 15 Minute Break)**
Subject:

❑ Daily Test Review Notes to Ace Tests
Start Time: _____ Finish Time: _____

❑ **Study Period 2**
Subject:

❑ Daily Test Review Notes to Ace Tests
Start Time: _____ Finish Time: _____

❑ **Study Period 3**
Subject:

❑ Daily Test Review Notes to Ace Tests
Start Time: _____ Finish Time: _____

❑ **Study Period 4**
Subject:

❑ Daily Test Review Notes to Ace Tests
Start Time: _____ Finish Time: _____

❑ **Study Period 5**
Subject:

❑ Daily Test Review Notes to Ace Tests
Start Time: _____ Finish Time: _____

Priority #1
Study for Test!

Priority #2
What's due tomorrow?

Priority #3
Math/Science?

Priority #4
English/History?

Priority #5
What time is dinner?

Priority #6
Write and Review: "My Daily Test Review Notes" to Ace Every Test Everytime!

Priority #7
Socialize with Family & Friends

Priority #8
Get Ready for Tomorrow!

Get Ready for Tomorrow:
❑ Pack Book Bag: Textbooks and Notebooks
❑ Checklist: Keys, School I.D., Wallet, Money, Pens, Pencils
❑ Check Weather (Umbrella?)
❑ Prepare School Clothing
❑ Charge Electronics
❑ Kiss Loved Ones
❑ Brush and Floss Teeth
❑ Set Alarm Clock

❑ **9-11 P.M. Regular Bedtime for Sleep Energy**

My Energy: Mind, Body and Spirit

Today's Positive Thoughts (My Self-Esteem Energy):

Today's Real Food Energy Choices:

Breakfast Energy: _____

Lunch Energy: _____

Dinner Energy: _____

Power Study Snacks: _____

Today's Exercise Energy (Break a Sweat!) : _____

Tonight's Regular Bedtime Energy: _____ P.M.

My Budget: Save, Spend, and Splurge

Total Amount: $ _____

Pay Yourself First: $ _____ My Savings

EXPENSES: NEEDS AND WANTS

Spend(Needs): $ _____

Splurge (Wants): $ _____

Total Expenses: $ _____

My Pocket Money: $ _____

My After School Family Chores

1.

2.

3.

My After School Activities

1.

2.

3.

My Journal of True Feelings

The Best Part of My Day:

The Worst Part of My Day:

❑ Great Day   ❑ Good Day   ❑ Stressful Day

My Homework Assignments

Today's Date:

My Homework: Read Chapter, Write Paper, Solve Problem, Ace Test

1st Assignment
Subject:
Due Date:

2nd Assignment
Subject:
Due Date:

3rd Assignment
Subject:
Due Date:

4th Assignment
Subject:
Due Date:

5th Assignment
Subject:
Due Date:

6th Assignment
Subject:
Due Date:

My Study Schedule

❏ **Study Period 1 (45 Minute Study & 15 Minute Break)**
Subject:
❏ **Daily Test Review Notes to Ace Tests**
Start Time: _____ Finish Time: _____

Priority #1
Study for Test!

Priority #2
What's due tomorrow?

❏ **Study Period 2**
Subject:
❏ **Daily Test Review Notes to Ace Tests**
Start Time: _____ Finish Time: _____

Priority #3
Math/Science?

Priority #4
English/History?

❏ **Study Period 3**
Subject:
❏ **Daily Test Review Notes to Ace Tests**
Start Time: _____ Finish Time: _____

Priority #5
What time is dinner?

Priority #6
Write and Review: "My Daily Test Review Notes" to Ace Every Test Everytime!

❏ **Study Period 4**
Subject:
❏ **Daily Test Review Notes to Ace Tests**
Start Time: _____ Finish Time: _____

Priority #7
Socialize with Family & Friends

Priority #8
Get Ready for Tomorrow!

❏ **Study Period 5**
Subject:
❏ **Daily Test Review Notes to Ace Tests**
Start Time: _____ Finish Time: _____

Get Ready for Tomorrow:
❏ Pack Book Bag: Textbooks and Notebooks
❏ Checklist: Keys, School I.D., Wallet, Money, Pens, Pencils
❏ Check Weather (Umbrella?)
❏ Prepare School Clothing
❏ Charge Electronics
❏ Kiss Loved Ones
❏ Brush and Floss Teeth
❏ Set Alarm Clock

❏ **9-11 P.M. Regular Bedtime for Sleep Energy**

My Energy: Mind, Body and Spirit

Today's Positive Thoughts (My Self-Esteem Energy):

Today's Real Food Energy Choices:

Breakfast Energy: _____

Lunch Energy: _____

Dinner Energy: _____

Power Study Snacks: _____

Today's Exercise Energy (Break a Sweat!) : _____

Tonight's Regular Bedtime Energy: _____ P.M.

My Budget: Save, Spend, and Splurge

Total Amount: $ _____

Pay Yourself First: $ _____ My Savings

EXPENSES: NEEDS AND WANTS

Spend(Needs): $ _____

Splurge (Wants): $ _____

Total Expenses: $ _____

My Pocket Money: $ _____

My After School Family Chores

1.

2.

3.

My After School Activities

1.

2.

3.

My Journal of True Feelings

The Best Part of My Day:

The Worst Part of My Day:

❑ Great Day   ❑ Good Day   ❑ Stressful Day

My Homework Assignments

Today's Date:

My Homework: Read Chapter, Write Paper, Solve Problem, Ace Test

1st Assignment
Subject:
Due Date:

2nd Assignment
Subject:
Due Date:

3rd Assignment
Subject:
Due Date:

4th Assignment
Subject:
Due Date:

5th Assignment
Subject:
Due Date:

6th Assignment
Subject:
Due Date:

My Study Schedule

❑ **Study Period 1 (45 Minute Study & 15 Minute Break)**
Subject:
❑ Daily Test Review Notes to Ace Tests
Start Time: _____   Finish Time: _____

❑ **Study Period 2**
Subject:
❑ Daily Test Review Notes to Ace Tests
Start Time: _____   Finish Time: _____

❑ **Study Period 3**
Subject:
❑ Daily Test Review Notes to Ace Tests
Start Time: _____   Finish Time: _____

❑ **Study Period 4**
Subject:
❑ Daily Test Review Notes to Ace Tests
Start Time: _____   Finish Time: _____

❑ **Study Period 5**
Subject:
❑ Daily Test Review Notes to Ace Tests
Start Time: _____   Finish Time: _____

Priority #1
Study for Test!

Priority #2
What's due tomorrow?

Priority #3
Math/Science?

Priority #4
English/History?

Priority #5
What time is dinner?

Priority #6
Write and Review: "My Daily Test Review Notes" to Ace Every Test Everytime!

Priority #7
Socialize with Family & Friends

Priority #8
Get Ready for Tomorrow!

Get Ready for Tomorrow:
❑ Pack Book Bag: Textbooks and Notebooks
❑ Checklist: Keys, School I.D., Wallet, Money, Pens, Pencils
❑ Check Weather (Umbrella?)
❑ Prepare School Clothing
❑ Charge Electronics
❑ Kiss Loved Ones
❑ Brush and Floss Teeth
❑ Set Alarm Clock

❑ **9-11 P.M. Regular Bedtime for Sleep Energy**

My Energy: Mind, Body and Spirit

Today's Positive Thoughts (My Self-Esteem Energy):

Today's Real Food Energy Choices:

Breakfast Energy: _____

Lunch Energy: _____

Dinner Energy: _____

Power Study Snacks: _____

Today's Exercise Energy (Break a Sweat!) : _____

Tonight's Regular Bedtime Energy: _____ P.M.

My Budget: Save, Spend, and Splurge

Total Amount: $ _____

Pay Yourself First: $ _____ My Savings

EXPENSES: NEEDS AND WANTS

Spend(Needs): $ _____

Splurge (Wants): $ _____

Total Expenses: $ _____

My Pocket Money: $ _____

My After School Family Chores

1.

2.

3.

My After School Activities

1.

2.

3.

My Journal of True Feelings

The Best Part of My Day:

The Worst Part of My Day:

❑ Great Day   ❑ Good Day   ❑ Stressful Day

My Homework Assignments

Today's Date:

My Homework: Read Chapter, Write Paper, Solve Problem, Ace Test

1st Assignment
Subject:
Due Date:

2nd Assignment
Subject:
Due Date:

3rd Assignment
Subject:
Due Date:

4th Assignment
Subject:
Due Date:

5th Assignment
Subject:
Due Date:

6th Assignment
Subject:
Due Date:

My Study Schedule

❑ **Study Period 1 (45 Minute Study & 15 Minute Break)**
Subject:
❑ Daily Test Review Notes to Ace Tests
Start Time: _____ Finish Time: _____

❑ **Study Period 2**
Subject:
❑ Daily Test Review Notes to Ace Tests
Start Time: _____ Finish Time: _____

❑ **Study Period 3**
Subject:
❑ Daily Test Review Notes to Ace Tests
Start Time: _____ Finish Time: _____

❑ **Study Period 4**
Subject:
❑ Daily Test Review Notes to Ace Tests
Start Time: _____ Finish Time: _____

❑ **Study Period 5**
Subject:
❑ Daily Test Review Notes to Ace Tests
Start Time: _____ Finish Time: _____

Priority #1
Study for Test!

Priority #2
What's due tomorrow?

Priority #3
Math/Science?

Priority #4
English/History?

Priority #5
What time is dinner?

Priority #6
Write and Review: "My Daily Test Review Notes" to Ace Every Test Everytime!

Priority #7
Socialize with Family & Friends

Priority #8
Get Ready for Tomorrow!

Get Ready for Tomorrow:
❑ Pack Book Bag: Textbooks and Notebooks
❑ Checklist: Keys, School I.D., Wallet, Money, Pens, Pencils
❑ Check Weather (Umbrella?)
❑ Prepare School Clothing
❑ Charge Electronics
❑ Kiss Loved Ones
❑ Brush and Floss Teeth
❑ Set Alarm Clock

❑ **9-11 P.M. Regular Bedtime for Sleep Energy**

My Energy: Mind, Body and Spirit

Today's Positive Thoughts (My Self-Esteem Energy):

Today's Real Food Energy Choices:

Breakfast Energy: _____

Lunch Energy: _____

Dinner Energy: _____

Power Study Snacks: _____

Today's Exercise Energy (Break a Sweat!) : _____

Tonight's Regular Bedtime Energy: _____ P.M.

My Budget: Save, Spend, and Splurge

Total Amount: $ _____

Pay Yourself First: $ _____ My Savings

EXPENSES: NEEDS AND WANTS

Spend(Needs): $ _____

Splurge (Wants): $ _____

Total Expenses: $ _____

My Pocket Money: $ _____

My After School Family Chores

1.

2.

3.

My After School Activities

1.

2.

3.

My Journal of True Feelings

The Best Part of My Day:

The Worst Part of My Day:

❏ Great Day   ❏ Good Day   ❏ Stressful Day

My Homework Assignments

Today's Date:

My Homework: Read Chapter, Write Paper, Solve Problem, Ace Test

1st Assignment
Subject:
Due Date:

2nd Assignment
Subject:
Due Date:

3rd Assignment
Subject:
Due Date:

4th Assignment
Subject:
Due Date:

5th Assignment
Subject:
Due Date:

6th Assignment
Subject:
Due Date:

My Study Schedule

❑ **Study Period 1 (45 Minute Study & 15 Minute Break)**
Subject:
❑ Daily Test Review Notes to Ace Tests
Start Time: _____   Finish Time: _____

——————————————————————————————

❑ **Study Period 2**
Subject:
❑ Daily Test Review Notes to Ace Tests
Start Time: _____   Finish Time: _____

——————————————————————————————

❑ **Study Period 3**
Subject:
❑ Daily Test Review Notes to Ace Tests
Start Time: _____   Finish Time: _____

——————————————————————————————

❑ **Study Period 4**
Subject:
❑ Daily Test Review Notes to Ace Tests
Start Time: _____   Finish Time: _____

——————————————————————————————

❑ **Study Period 5**
Subject:
❑ Daily Test Review Notes to Ace Tests
Start Time: _____   Finish Time: _____

——————————————————————————————

Priority #1
Study for Test!

Priority #2
What's due tomorrow?

Priority #3
Math/Science?

Priority #4
English/History?

Priority #5
What time is dinner?

Priority #6
Write and Review: "My Daily Test Review Notes" to Ace Every Test Everytime!

Priority #7
Socialize with Family & Friends

Priority #8
Get Ready for Tomorrow!

Get Ready for Tomorrow:
❑ Pack Book Bag: Textbooks and Notebooks
❑ Checklist: Keys, School I.D., Wallet, Money, Pens, Pencils
❑ Check Weather (Umbrella?)
❑ Prepare School Clothing
❑ Charge Electronics
❑ Kiss Loved Ones
❑ Brush and Floss Teeth
❑ Set Alarm Clock

❑ **9-11 P.M. Regular Bedtime for Sleep Energy**

My Energy: Mind, Body and Spirit

Today's Positive Thoughts (My Self-Esteem Energy):

_____

_____

Today's Real Food Energy Choices:

Breakfast Energy: _____

Lunch Energy: _____

Dinner Energy: _____

Power Study Snacks: _____

_____

Today's Exercise Energy (Break a Sweat!) : _____

Tonight's Regular Bedtime Energy: _____ P.M.

_____

My Budget: Save, Spend, and Splurge

Total Amount: $ _____

Pay Yourself First: $ _____ My Savings

EXPENSES: NEEDS AND WANTS

Spend(Needs): $ _____

Splurge (Wants): $ _____

Total Expenses: $ _____

My Pocket Money: $ _____

My After School Family Chores

1.

2.

3.

My After School Activities

1.

2.

3.

My Journal of True Feelings

The Best Part of My Day:

The Worst Part of My Day:

❏ Great Day   ❏ Good Day   ❏ Stressful Day

My Homework Assignments

Today's Date:

My Homework: Read Chapter, Write Paper, Solve Problem, Ace Test

1st Assignment
Subject:
Due Date:

2nd Assignment
Subject:
Due Date:

3rd Assignment
Subject:
Due Date:

4th Assignment
Subject:
Due Date:

5th Assignment
Subject:
Due Date:

6th Assignment
Subject:
Due Date:

My Study Schedule

❑ **Study Period 1 (45 Minute Study & 15 Minute Break)**
Subject:
❑ Daily Test Review Notes to Ace Tests
Start Time: _____ Finish Time: _____

❑ **Study Period 2**
Subject:
❑ Daily Test Review Notes to Ace Tests
Start Time: _____ Finish Time: _____

❑ **Study Period 3**
Subject:
❑ Daily Test Review Notes to Ace Tests
Start Time: _____ Finish Time: _____

❑ **Study Period 4**
Subject:
❑ Daily Test Review Notes to Ace Tests
Start Time: _____ Finish Time: _____

❑ **Study Period 5**
Subject:
❑ Daily Test Review Notes to Ace Tests
Start Time: _____ Finish Time: _____

Priority #1
Study for Test!

Priority #2
What's due tomorrow?

Priority #3
Math/Science?

Priority #4
English/History?

Priority #5
What time is dinner?

Priority #6
Write and Review: "My Daily Test Review Notes" to Ace Every Test Everytime!

Priority #7
Socialize with Family & Friends

Priority #8
Get Ready for Tomorrow!

Get Ready for Tomorrow:
❑ Pack Book Bag: Textbooks and Notebooks
❑ Checklist: Keys, School I.D., Wallet, Money, Pens, Pencils
❑ Check Weather (Umbrella?)
❑ Prepare School Clothing
❑ Charge Electronics
❑ Kiss Loved Ones
❑ Brush and Floss Teeth
❑ Set Alarm Clock

❑ **9-11 P.M. Regular Bedtime for Sleep Energy**

My Energy: Mind, Body and Spirit

Today's Positive Thoughts (My Self-Esteem Energy):

Today's Real Food Energy Choices:

Breakfast Energy: _____

Lunch Energy: _____

Dinner Energy: _____

Power Study Snacks: _____

Today's Exercise Energy (Break a Sweat!) : _____

Tonight's Regular Bedtime Energy: _____ P.M.

My Budget: Save, Spend, and Splurge

Total Amount: $ _____

Pay Yourself First: $ _____ My Savings

EXPENSES: NEEDS AND WANTS

Spend(Needs): $ _____

Splurge (Wants): $ _____

Total Expenses: $ _____

My Pocket Money: $ _____

My After School Family Chores

1.

2.

3.

My After School Activities

1.

2.

3.

My Journal of True Feelings

The Best Part of My Day:

The Worst Part of My Day:

❏ Great Day　　❏ Good Day　　❏ Stressful Day

My Homework Assignments

Today's Date:

My Homework: Read Chapter, Write Paper, Solve Problem, Ace Test

1st Assignment
Subject:
Due Date:

2nd Assignment
Subject:
Due Date:

3rd Assignment
Subject:
Due Date:

4th Assignment
Subject:
Due Date:

5th Assignment
Subject:
Due Date:

6th Assignment
Subject:
Due Date:

My Study Schedule

❏ **Study Period 1 (45 Minute Study & 15 Minute Break)**
Subject:
❏ Daily Test Review Notes to Ace Tests
Start Time: _____ Finish Time: _____

❏ **Study Period 2**
Subject:
❏ Daily Test Review Notes to Ace Tests
Start Time: _____ Finish Time: _____

❏ **Study Period 3**
Subject:
❏ Daily Test Review Notes to Ace Tests
Start Time: _____ Finish Time: _____

❏ **Study Period 4**
Subject:
❏ Daily Test Review Notes to Ace Tests
Start Time: _____ Finish Time: _____

❏ **Study Period 5**
Subject:
❏ Daily Test Review Notes to Ace Tests
Start Time: _____ Finish Time: _____

Priority #1
Study for Test!

Priority #2
What's due tomorrow?

Priority #3
Math/Science?

Priority #4
English/History?

Priority #5
What time is dinner?

Priority #6
Write and Review: "My Daily Test Review Notes" to Ace Every Test Everytime!

Priority #7
Socialize with Family & Friends

Priority #8
Get Ready for Tomorrow!

Get Ready for Tomorrow:
❏ Pack Book Bag: Textbooks and Notebooks
❏ Checklist: Keys, School I.D., Wallet, Money, Pens, Pencils
❏ Check Weather (Umbrella?)
❏ Prepare School Clothing
❏ Charge Electronics
❏ Kiss Loved Ones
❏ Brush and Floss Teeth
❏ Set Alarm Clock

❏ **9-11 P.M. Regular Bedtime for Sleep Energy**

My Energy: Mind, Body and Spirit

Today's Positive Thoughts (My Self-Esteem Energy):

Today's Real Food Energy Choices:

Breakfast Energy: _____

Lunch Energy: _____

Dinner Energy: _____

Power Study Snacks: _____

Today's Exercise Energy (Break a Sweat!) : _____

Tonight's Regular Bedtime Energy: _____ P.M.

My Budget: Save, Spend, and Splurge

Total Amount: $ _____

Pay Yourself First: $ _____ My Savings

EXPENSES: NEEDS AND WANTS

Spend(Needs): $ _____

Splurge (Wants): $ _____

Total Expenses: $ _____

My Pocket Money: $ _____

My After School Family Chores

1.

2.

3.

_____

My After School Activities

1.

2.

3.

_____

My Journal of True Feelings

The Best Part of My Day:

The Worst Part of My Day:

❑ Great Day   ❑ Good Day   ❑ Stressful Day

My Homework Assignments

Today's Date:

My Homework: Read Chapter, Write Paper, Solve Problem, Ace Test

1st Assignment
Subject:
Due Date:

2nd Assignment
Subject:
Due Date:

3rd Assignment
Subject:
Due Date:

4th Assignment
Subject:
Due Date:

5th Assignment
Subject:
Due Date:

6th Assignment
Subject:
Due Date:

My Study Schedule

❑ Study Period 1 (45 Minute Study & 15 Minute Break)
Subject:

❑ Daily Test Review Notes to Ace Tests
Start Time: _____ Finish Time: _____

❑ Study Period 2
Subject:

❑ Daily Test Review Notes to Ace Tests
Start Time: _____ Finish Time: _____

❑ Study Period 3
Subject:

❑ Daily Test Review Notes to Ace Tests
Start Time: _____ Finish Time: _____

❑ Study Period 4
Subject:

❑ Daily Test Review Notes to Ace Tests
Start Time: _____ Finish Time: _____

❑ Study Period 5
Subject:

❑ Daily Test Review Notes to Ace Tests
Start Time: _____ Finish Time: _____

Priority #1
Study for Test!

Priority #2
What's due tomorrow?

Priority #3
Math/Science?

Priority #4
English/History?

Priority #5
What time is dinner?

Priority #6
Write and Review: "My Daily Test Review Notes" to Ace Every Test Everytime!

Priority #7
Socialize with Family & Friends

Priority #8
Get Ready for Tomorrow!

Get Ready for Tomorrow:
❑ Pack Book Bag: Textbooks and Notebooks
❑ Checklist: Keys, School I.D., Wallet, Money, Pens, Pencils
❑ Check Weather (Umbrella?)
❑ Prepare School Clothing
❑ Charge Electronics
❑ Kiss Loved Ones
❑ Brush and Floss Teeth
❑ Set Alarm Clock

❑ 9-11 P.M. Regular Bedtime for Sleep Energy

My Energy: Mind, Body and Spirit

Today's Positive Thoughts (My Self-Esteem Energy):

Today's Real Food Energy Choices:

Breakfast Energy: _____

Lunch Energy: _____

Dinner Energy: _____

Power Study Snacks: _____

Today's Exercise Energy (Break a Sweat!) : _____

Tonight's Regular Bedtime Energy: _____ P.M.

My Budget: Save, Spend, and Splurge

Total Amount: $ _____

Pay Yourself First: $ _____ My Savings

EXPENSES: NEEDS AND WANTS

Spend(Needs): $ _____

Splurge (Wants): $ _____

Total Expenses: $ _____

My Pocket Money: $ _____

My After School Family Chores

1.

2.

3.

My After School Activities

1.

2.

3.

My Journal of True Feelings

The Best Part of My Day:

The Worst Part of My Day:

❑ Great Day ❑ Good Day ❑ Stressful Day

My Homework Assignments

Today's Date:

My Homework: Read Chapter, Write Paper, Solve Problem, Ace Test

1st Assignment
Subject:
Due Date:

2nd Assignment
Subject:
Due Date:

3rd Assignment
Subject:
Due Date:

4th Assignment
Subject:
Due Date:

5th Assignment
Subject:
Due Date:

6th Assignment
Subject:
Due Date:

My Study Schedule

❑ **Study Period 1 (45 Minute Study & 15 Minute Break)**
Subject:
❑ Daily Test Review Notes to Ace Tests
Start Time: _____ Finish Time: _____

❑ **Study Period 2**
Subject:
❑ Daily Test Review Notes to Ace Tests
Start Time: _____ Finish Time: _____

❑ **Study Period 3**
Subject:
❑ Daily Test Review Notes to Ace Tests
Start Time: _____ Finish Time: _____

❑ **Study Period 4**
Subject:
❑ Daily Test Review Notes to Ace Tests
Start Time: _____ Finish Time: _____

❑ **Study Period 5**
Subject:
❑ Daily Test Review Notes to Ace Tests
Start Time: _____ Finish Time: _____

Priority #1
Study for Test!

Priority #2
What's due tomorrow?

Priority #3
Math/Science?

Priority #4
English/History?

Priority #5
What time is dinner?

Priority #6
Write and Review: "My Daily Test Review Notes" to Ace Every Test Everytime!

Priority #7
Socialize with Family & Friends

Priority #8
Get Ready for Tomorrow!

Get Ready for Tomorrow:
❑ Pack Book Bag: Textbooks and Notebooks
❑ Checklist: Keys, School I.D., Wallet, Money, Pens, Pencils
❑ Check Weather (Umbrella?)
❑ Prepare School Clothing
❑ Charge Electronics
❑ Kiss Loved Ones
❑ Brush and Floss Teeth
❑ Set Alarm Clock

❑ **9-11 P.M. Regular Bedtime for Sleep Energy**

My Energy: Mind, Body and Spirit

Today's Positive Thoughts (My Self-Esteem Energy):

Today's Real Food Energy Choices:

Breakfast Energy: _____

Lunch Energy: _____

Dinner Energy: _____

Power Study Snacks: _____

Today's Exercise Energy (Break a Sweat!) : _____

Tonight's Regular Bedtime Energy: _____ P.M.

My Budget: Save, Spend, and Splurge

Total Amount: $ _____

Pay Yourself First: $ _____ My Savings

EXPENSES: NEEDS AND WANTS

Spend(Needs): $ _____

Splurge (Wants): $ _____

Total Expenses: $ _____

My Pocket Money: $ _____

My After School Family Chores

1.

2.

3.

My After School Activities

1.

2.

3.

My Journal of True Feelings

The Best Part of My Day:

The Worst Part of My Day:

❏ Great Day   ❏ Good Day   ❏ Stressful Day

My Homework Assignments

Today's Date:

My Homework: Read Chapter, Write Paper, Solve Problem, Ace Test

1st Assignment
Subject:
Due Date:

2nd Assignment
Subject:
Due Date:

3rd Assignment
Subject:
Due Date:

4th Assignment
Subject:
Due Date:

5th Assignment
Subject:
Due Date:

6th Assignment
Subject:
Due Date:

My Study Schedule

❏ **Study Period 1 (45 Minute Study & 15 Minute Break)**
Subject:
❏ Daily Test Review Notes to Ace Tests
Start Time: _____ Finish Time: _____

❏ **Study Period 2**
Subject:
❏ Daily Test Review Notes to Ace Tests
Start Time: _____ Finish Time: _____

❏ **Study Period 3**
Subject:
❏ Daily Test Review Notes to Ace Tests
Start Time: _____ Finish Time: _____

❏ **Study Period 4**
Subject:
❏ Daily Test Review Notes to Ace Tests
Start Time: _____ Finish Time: _____

❏ **Study Period 5**
Subject:
❏ Daily Test Review Notes to Ace Tests
Start Time: _____ Finish Time: _____

Priority #1
Study for Test!

Priority #2
What's due tomorrow?

Priority #3
Math/Science?

Priority #4
English/History?

Priority #5
What time is dinner?

Priority #6
Write and Review: "My Daily Test Review Notes" to Ace Every Test Everytime!

Priority #7
Socialize with Family & Friends

Priority #8
Get Ready for Tomorrow!

Get Ready for Tomorrow:
❏ Pack Book Bag: Textbooks and Notebooks
❏ Checklist: Keys, School I.D., Wallet, Money, Pens, Pencils
❏ Check Weather (Umbrella?)
❏ Prepare School Clothing
❏ Charge Electronics
❏ Kiss Loved Ones
❏ Brush and Floss Teeth
❏ Set Alarm Clock

❏ 9-11 P.M. Regular Bedtime for Sleep Energy

My Energy: Mind, Body and Spirit

Today's Positive Thoughts (My Self-Esteem Energy):

Today's Real Food Energy Choices:

Breakfast Energy: _____

Lunch Energy: _____

Dinner Energy: _____

Power Study Snacks: _____

Today's Exercise Energy (Break a Sweat!) : _____

Tonight's Regular Bedtime Energy: _____ P.M.

My Budget: Save, Spend, and Splurge

Total Amount: $ _____

Pay Yourself First: $ _____ My Savings

EXPENSES: NEEDS AND WANTS

Spend(Needs): $ _____

Splurge (Wants): $ _____

Total Expenses: $ _____

My Pocket Money: $ _____

My After School Family Chores

1.

2.

3.

My After School Activities

1.

2.

3.

My Journal of True Feelings

The Best Part of My Day:

The Worst Part of My Day:

❏ Great Day   ❏ Good Day   ❏ Stressful Day

My Homework Assignments

Today's Date:

My Homework: Read Chapter, Write Paper, Solve Problem, Ace Test

1st Assignment
Subject:
Due Date:

2nd Assignment
Subject:
Due Date:

3rd Assignment
Subject:
Due Date:

4th Assignment
Subject:
Due Date:

5th Assignment
Subject:
Due Date:

6th Assignment
Subject:
Due Date:

My Study Schedule

❏ Study Period 1 (45 Minute Study & 15 Minute Break)
Subject:

❏ Daily Test Review Notes to Ace Tests
Start Time: _____ Finish Time: _____

❏ Study Period 2
Subject:

❏ Daily Test Review Notes to Ace Tests
Start Time: _____ Finish Time: _____

❏ Study Period 3
Subject:

❏ Daily Test Review Notes to Ace Tests
Start Time: _____ Finish Time: _____

❏ Study Period 4
Subject:

❏ Daily Test Review Notes to Ace Tests
Start Time: _____ Finish Time: _____

❏ Study Period 5
Subject:

❏ Daily Test Review Notes to Ace Tests
Start Time: _____ Finish Time: _____

Priority #1
Study for Test!

Priority #2
What's due
tomorrow?

Priority #3
Math/Science?

Priority #4
English/History?

Priority #5
What time is
dinner?

Priority #6
Write and Review:
"My Daily Test
Review Notes" to
Ace Every Test
Everytime!

Priority #7
Socialize with
Family & Friends

Priority #8
Get Ready for
Tomorrow!

Get Ready for Tomorrow:
❏ Pack Book Bag: Textbooks and Notebooks
❏ Checklist: Keys, School I.D., Wallet, Money, Pens, Pencils
❏ Check Weather (Umbrella?)
❏ Prepare School Clothing
❏ Charge Electronics
❏ Kiss Loved Ones
❏ Brush and Floss Teeth
❏ Set Alarm Clock

❏ 9-11 P.M. Regular Bedtime for Sleep Energy

My Energy: Mind, Body and Spirit

Today's Positive Thoughts (My Self-Esteem Energy):

Today's Real Food Energy Choices:

Breakfast Energy: _____

Lunch Energy: _____

Dinner Energy: _____

Power Study Snacks: _____

Today's Exercise Energy (Break a Sweat!) : _____

Tonight's Regular Bedtime Energy: _____ P.M.

My Budget: Save, Spend, and Splurge

Total Amount: $ _____

Pay Yourself First: $ _____ My Savings

EXPENSES: NEEDS AND WANTS

Spend(Needs): $ _____

Splurge (Wants): $ _____

Total Expenses: $ _____

My Pocket Money: $ _____

My After School Family Chores

1.

2.

3.

_____

My After School Activities

1.

2.

3.

_____

My Journal of True Feelings

The Best Part of My Day:

The Worst Part of My Day:

❏ Great Day   ❏ Good Day   ❏ Stressful Day

My Homework Assignments

Today's Date:

My Homework: Read Chapter, Write Paper, Solve Problem, Ace Test

1st Assignment
Subject:
Due Date:

2nd Assignment
Subject:
Due Date:

3rd Assignment
Subject:
Due Date:

4th Assignment
Subject:
Due Date:

5th Assignment
Subject:
Due Date:

6th Assignment
Subject:
Due Date:

My Study Schedule

❑ **Study Period 1 (45 Minute Study & 15 Minute Break)**
Subject:
❑ Daily Test Review Notes to Ace Tests
Start Time: _____ Finish Time: _____

❑ **Study Period 2**
Subject:
❑ Daily Test Review Notes to Ace Tests
Start Time: _____ Finish Time: _____

❑ **Study Period 3**
Subject:
❑ Daily Test Review Notes to Ace Tests
Start Time: _____ Finish Time: _____

❑ **Study Period 4**
Subject:
❑ Daily Test Review Notes to Ace Tests
Start Time: _____ Finish Time: _____

❑ **Study Period 5**
Subject:
❑ Daily Test Review Notes to Ace Tests
Start Time: _____ Finish Time: _____

Priority #1
Study for Test!

Priority #2
What's due tomorrow?

Priority #3
Math/Science?

Priority #4
English/History?

Priority #5
What time is dinner?

Priority #6
Write and Review: "My Daily Test Review Notes" to Ace Every Test Everytime!

Priority #7
Socialize with Family & Friends

Priority #8
Get Ready for Tomorrow!

Get Ready for Tomorrow:
❑ Pack Book Bag: Textbooks and Notebooks
❑ Checklist: Keys, School I.D., Wallet, Money, Pens, Pencils
❑ Check Weather (Umbrella?)
❑ Prepare School Clothing
❑ Charge Electronics
❑ Kiss Loved Ones
❑ Brush and Floss Teeth
❑ Set Alarm Clock

❑ **9-11 P.M. Regular Bedtime for Sleep Energy**

My Energy: Mind, Body and Spirit

Today's Positive Thoughts (My Self-Esteem Energy):

_____

_____

Today's Real Food Energy Choices:

Breakfast Energy: _____

Lunch Energy: _____

Dinner Energy: _____

Power Study Snacks: _____

_____

Today's Exercise Energy (Break a Sweat!) : _____

Tonight's Regular Bedtime Energy: _____ P.M.

_____

My Budget: Save, Spend, and Splurge

Total Amount: $ _____

Pay Yourself First: $ _____ My Savings

EXPENSES: NEEDS AND WANTS

Spend(Needs): $ _____

Splurge (Wants): $ _____

Total Expenses: $ _____

My Pocket Money: $ _____

My After School Family Chores

1.

2.

3.

My After School Activities

1.

2.

3.

My Journal of True Feelings

The Best Part of My Day:

The Worst Part of My Day:

❑ Great Day   ❑ Good Day   ❑ Stressful Day

My Homework Assignments

Today's Date:

My Homework: Read Chapter, Write Paper, Solve Problem, Ace Test

1st Assignment
Subject:
Due Date:

2nd Assignment
Subject:
Due Date:

3rd Assignment
Subject:
Due Date:

4th Assignment
Subject:
Due Date:

5th Assignment
Subject:
Due Date:

6th Assignment
Subject:
Due Date:

My Study Schedule

❑ **Study Period 1 (45 Minute Study & 15 Minute Break)**
Subject:
❑ Daily Test Review Notes to Ace Tests
Start Time: _____ Finish Time: _____

❑ **Study Period 2**
Subject:
❑ Daily Test Review Notes to Ace Tests
Start Time: _____ Finish Time: _____

❑ **Study Period 3**
Subject:
❑ Daily Test Review Notes to Ace Tests
Start Time: _____ Finish Time: _____

❑ **Study Period 4**
Subject:
❑ Daily Test Review Notes to Ace Tests
Start Time: _____ Finish Time: _____

❑ **Study Period 5**
Subject:
❑ Daily Test Review Notes to Ace Tests
Start Time: _____ Finish Time: _____

Priority #1
Study for Test!

Priority #2
What's due tomorrow?

Priority #3
Math/Science?

Priority #4
English/History?

Priority #5
What time is dinner?

Priority #6
Write and Review: "My Daily Test Review Notes" to Ace Every Test Everytime!

Priority #7
Socialize with Family & Friends

Priority #8
Get Ready for Tomorrow!

Get Ready for Tomorrow:
❑ Pack Book Bag: Textbooks and Notebooks
❑ Checklist: Keys, School I.D., Wallet, Money, Pens, Pencils
❑ Check Weather (Umbrella?)
❑ Prepare School Clothing
❑ Charge Electronics
❑ Kiss Loved Ones
❑ Brush and Floss Teeth
❑ Set Alarm Clock

❑ **9–11 P.M. Regular Bedtime for Sleep Energy**

My Energy: Mind, Body and Spirit

Today's Positive Thoughts (My Self-Esteem Energy):

Today's Real Food Energy Choices:

Breakfast Energy: _____

Lunch Energy: _____

Dinner Energy: _____

Power Study Snacks: _____

Today's Exercise Energy (Break a Sweat!) : _____

Tonight's Regular Bedtime Energy: _____ P.M.

My Budget: Save, Spend, and Splurge

Total Amount: $ _____

Pay Yourself First: $ _____ My Savings

EXPENSES: NEEDS AND WANTS

Spend(Needs): $ _____

Splurge (Wants): $ _____

Total Expenses: $ _____

My Pocket Money: $ _____

My After School Family Chores

1.

2.

3.

My After School Activities

1.

2.

3.

My Journal of True Feelings

The Best Part of My Day:

The Worst Part of My Day:

❏ Great Day   ❏ Good Day   ❏ Stressful Day

My Homework Assignments

Today's Date:

My Homework: Read Chapter, Write Paper, Solve Problem, Ace Test

1st Assignment
Subject:
Due Date:

2nd Assignment
Subject:
Due Date:

3rd Assignment
Subject:
Due Date:

4th Assignment
Subject:
Due Date:

5th Assignment
Subject:
Due Date:

6th Assignment
Subject:
Due Date:

My Study Schedule

❑ **Study Period 1 (45 Minute Study & 15 Minute Break)**
Subject:

❑ Daily Test Review Notes to Ace Tests
Start Time: _____ Finish Time: _____

❑ **Study Period 2**
Subject:

❑ Daily Test Review Notes to Ace Tests
Start Time: _____ Finish Time: _____

❑ **Study Period 3**
Subject:

❑ Daily Test Review Notes to Ace Tests
Start Time: _____ Finish Time: _____

❑ **Study Period 4**
Subject:

❑ Daily Test Review Notes to Ace Tests
Start Time: _____ Finish Time: _____

❑ **Study Period 5**
Subject:

❑ Daily Test Review Notes to Ace Tests
Start Time: _____ Finish Time: _____

Priority #1
Study for Test!

Priority #2
What's due tomorrow?

Priority #3
Math/Science?

Priority #4
English/History?

Priority #5
What time is dinner?

Priority #6
Write and Review: "My Daily Test Review Notes" to Ace Every Test Everytime!

Priority #7
Socialize with Family & Friends

Priority #8
Get Ready for Tomorrow!

Get Ready for Tomorrow:
❑ Pack Book Bag: Textbooks and Notebooks
❑ Checklist: Keys, School I.D., Wallet, Money, Pens, Pencils
❑ Check Weather (Umbrella?)
❑ Prepare School Clothing
❑ Charge Electronics
❑ Kiss Loved Ones
❑ Brush and Floss Teeth
❑ Set Alarm Clock

❑ **9-11 P.M. Regular Bedtime for Sleep Energy**

My Energy: Mind, Body and Spirit

Today's Positive Thoughts (My Self-Esteem Energy):

Today's Real Food Energy Choices:

Breakfast Energy: _____

Lunch Energy: _____

Dinner Energy: _____

Power Study Snacks: _____

Today's Exercise Energy (Break a Sweat!) : _____

Tonight's Regular Bedtime Energy: _____ P.M.

My Budget: Save, Spend, and Splurge

Total Amount: $ _____

Pay Yourself First: $ _____ My Savings

EXPENSES: NEEDS AND WANTS

Spend(Needs): $ _____

Splurge (Wants): $ _____

Total Expenses: $ _____

My Pocket Money: $ _____

My After School Family Chores

1.

2.

3.

My After School Activities

1.

2.

3.

My Journal of True Feelings

The Best Part of My Day:

The Worst Part of My Day:

❏ Great Day   ❏ Good Day   ❏ Stressful Day

My Homework Assignments

Today's Date:

My Homework: Read Chapter, Write Paper, Solve Problem, Ace Test

1st Assignment
Subject:
Due Date:

2nd Assignment
Subject:
Due Date:

3rd Assignment
Subject:
Due Date:

4th Assignment
Subject:
Due Date:

5th Assignment
Subject:
Due Date:

6th Assignment
Subject:
Due Date:

My Study Schedule

❏ **Study Period 1 (45 Minute Study & 15 Minute Break)**
Subject:
❏ **Daily Test Review Notes to Ace Tests**
Start Time: _____ Finish Time: _____

❏ **Study Period 2**
Subject:
❏ **Daily Test Review Notes to Ace Tests**
Start Time: _____ Finish Time: _____

❏ **Study Period 3**
Subject:
❏ **Daily Test Review Notes to Ace Tests**
Start Time: _____ Finish Time: _____

❏ **Study Period 4**
Subject:
❏ **Daily Test Review Notes to Ace Tests**
Start Time: _____ Finish Time: _____

❏ **Study Period 5**
Subject:
❏ **Daily Test Review Notes to Ace Tests**
Start Time: _____ Finish Time: _____

Priority #1
Study for Test!

Priority #2
What's due tomorrow?

Priority #3
Math/Science?

Priority #4
English/History?

Priority #5
What time is dinner?

Priority #6
Write and Review: "My Daily Test Review Notes" to Ace Every Test Everytime!

Priority #7
Socialize with Family & Friends

Priority #8
Get Ready for Tomorrow!

Get Ready for Tomorrow:
❏ Pack Book Bag: Textbooks and Notebooks
❏ Checklist: Keys, School I.D., Wallet, Money, Pens, Pencils
❏ Check Weather (Umbrella?)
❏ Prepare School Clothing
❏ Charge Electronics
❏ Kiss Loved Ones
❏ Brush and Floss Teeth
❏ Set Alarm Clock

❏ **9-11 P.M. Regular Bedtime for Sleep Energy**

My Energy: Mind, Body and Spirit

Today's Positive Thoughts (My Self-Esteem Energy):

_____

_____

Today's Real Food Energy Choices:

Breakfast Energy: _____

Lunch Energy: _____

Dinner Energy: _____

Power Study Snacks: _____

_____

Today's Exercise Energy (Break a Sweat!) : _____

Tonight's Regular Bedtime Energy: _____ P.M.

_____

My Budget: Save, Spend, and Splurge

Total Amount: $ _____

Pay Yourself First: $ _____ My Savings

EXPENSES: NEEDS AND WANTS

Spend(Needs): $ _____

Splurge (Wants): $ _____

Total Expenses: $ _____

My Pocket Money: $ _____

My After School Family Chores

1.

2.

3.

My After School Activities

1.

2.

3.

My Journal of True Feelings

The Best Part of My Day:

The Worst Part of My Day:

❑ Great Day   ❑ Good Day   ❑ Stressful Day

My Homework Assignments

Today's Date:

My Homework: Read Chapter, Write Paper, Solve Problem, Ace Test

1st Assignment
Subject:
Due Date:

2nd Assignment
Subject:
Due Date:

3rd Assignment
Subject:
Due Date:

4th Assignment
Subject:
Due Date:

5th Assignment
Subject:
Due Date:

6th Assignment
Subject:
Due Date:

My Study Schedule

❑ **Study Period 1 (45 Minute Study & 15 Minute Break)**
Subject:
❑ Daily Test Review Notes to Ace Tests
Start Time: _____ Finish Time: _____

❑ **Study Period 2**
Subject:
❑ Daily Test Review Notes to Ace Tests
Start Time: _____ Finish Time: _____

❑ **Study Period 3**
Subject:
❑ Daily Test Review Notes to Ace Tests
Start Time: _____ Finish Time: _____

❑ **Study Period 4**
Subject:
❑ Daily Test Review Notes to Ace Tests
Start Time: _____ Finish Time: _____

❑ **Study Period 5**
Subject:
❑ Daily Test Review Notes to Ace Tests
Start Time: _____ Finish Time: _____

Priority #1
Study for Test!

Priority #2
What's due tomorrow?

Priority #3
Math/Science?

Priority #4
English/History?

Priority #5
What time is dinner?

Priority #6
Write and Review: "My Daily Test Review Notes" to Ace Every Test Everytime!

Priority #7
Socialize with Family & Friends

Priority #8
Get Ready for Tomorrow!

Get Ready for Tomorrow:
❑ Pack Book Bag: Textbooks and Notebooks
❑ Checklist: Keys, School I.D., Wallet, Money, Pens, Pencils
❑ Check Weather (Umbrella?)
❑ Prepare School Clothing
❑ Charge Electronics
❑ Kiss Loved Ones
❑ Brush and Floss Teeth
❑ Set Alarm Clock

❑ **9–11 P.M. Regular Bedtime for Sleep Energy**

My Energy: Mind, Body and Spirit

Today's Positive Thoughts (My Self-Esteem Energy):

_____

_____

Today's Real Food Energy Choices:

Breakfast Energy: _____

Lunch Energy: _____

Dinner Energy: _____

Power Study Snacks: _____

_____

Today's Exercise Energy (Break a Sweat!) : _____

Tonight's Regular Bedtime Energy: _____ P.M.

_____

My Budget: Save, Spend, and Splurge

Total Amount: $ _____

Pay Yourself First: $ _____ My Savings

EXPENSES: NEEDS AND WANTS

Spend(Needs): $ _____

Splurge (Wants): $ _____

Total Expenses: $ _____

My Pocket Money: $ _____

My After School Family Chores

1.

2.

3.

My After School Activities

1.

2.

3.

My Journal of True Feelings

The Best Part of My Day:

The Worst Part of My Day:

❏ Great Day   ❏ Good Day   ❏ Stressful Day

My Homework Assignments

Today's Date:

My Homework: Read Chapter, Write Paper, Solve Problem, Ace Test

1st Assignment
Subject:
Due Date:

2nd Assignment
Subject:
Due Date:

3rd Assignment
Subject:
Due Date:

4th Assignment
Subject:
Due Date:

5th Assignment
Subject:
Due Date:

6th Assignment
Subject:
Due Date:

My Study Schedule

❑ **Study Period 1 (45 Minute Study & 15 Minute Break)**
Subject:
❑ Daily Test Review Notes to Ace Tests
Start Time: _____ Finish Time: _____

❑ **Study Period 2**
Subject:
❑ Daily Test Review Notes to Ace Tests
Start Time: _____ Finish Time: _____

❑ **Study Period 3**
Subject:
❑ Daily Test Review Notes to Ace Tests
Start Time: _____ Finish Time: _____

❑ **Study Period 4**
Subject:
❑ Daily Test Review Notes to Ace Tests
Start Time: _____ Finish Time: _____

❑ **Study Period 5**
Subject:
❑ Daily Test Review Notes to Ace Tests
Start Time: _____ Finish Time: _____

Priority #1
Study for Test!

Priority #2
What's due tomorrow?

Priority #3
Math/Science?

Priority #4
English/History?

Priority #5
What time is dinner?

Priority #6
Write and Review: "My Daily Test Review Notes" to Ace Every Test Everytime!

Priority #7
Socialize with Family & Friends

Priority #8
Get Ready for Tomorrow!

Get Ready for Tomorrow:
❑ Pack Book Bag: Textbooks and Notebooks
❑ Checklist: Keys, School I.D., Wallet, Money, Pens, Pencils
❑ Check Weather (Umbrella?)
❑ Prepare School Clothing
❑ Charge Electronics
❑ Kiss Loved Ones
❑ Brush and Floss Teeth
❑ Set Alarm Clock

❑ **9-11 P.M. Regular Bedtime for Sleep Energy**

My Energy: Mind, Body and Spirit

Today's Positive Thoughts (My Self-Esteem Energy):

Today's Real Food Energy Choices:

Breakfast Energy: _____

Lunch Energy: _____

Dinner Energy: _____

Power Study Snacks: _____

Today's Exercise Energy (Break a Sweat!) : _____

Tonight's Regular Bedtime Energy: _____ P.M.

My Budget: Save, Spend, and Splurge

Total Amount: $ _____

Pay Yourself First: $ _____ My Savings

EXPENSES: NEEDS AND WANTS

Spend(Needs): $ _____

Splurge (Wants): $ _____

Total Expenses: $ _____

My Pocket Money: $ _____

My After School Family Chores

1.

2.

3.

My After School Activities

1.

2.

3.

My Journal of True Feelings

The Best Part of My Day:

The Worst Part of My Day:

❏ Great Day   ❏ Good Day   ❏ Stressful Day

Keep Track of Grades

Class:

Tests/Quizzes:

Essays/Papers:

Projects:

Final Grade:

Good Grades Deserve Great Rewards:

Class:

Tests/Quizzes:

Essays/Papers:

Projects:

Final Grade:

Good Grades Deserve Great Rewards:

Class:

Tests/Quizzes:

Essays/Papers:

Projects:

Final Grade:

Good Grades Deserve Great Rewards:

Class:

Tests/Quizzes:

Essays/Papers:

Projects:

Final Grade:

Good Grades Deserve Great Rewards:

Good Grades Deserve Great Rewards

Class:

Tests/Quizzes:

Essays/Papers:

Projects:

Final Grade:

Good Grades Deserve Great Rewards:

Class:

Tests/Quizzes:

Essays/Papers:

Projects:

Final Grade:

Good Grades Deserve Great Rewards:

Class:

Tests/Quizzes:

Essays/Papers:

Projects:

Final Grade:

Good Grades Deserve Great Rewards:

Class:

Tests/Quizzes:

Essays/Papers:

Projects:

Final Grade:

Good Grades Deserve Great Rewards:

My Teacher Contacts

Class:
Teacher:
Office Hours:
Phone Number:
Email:
Teacher's Pet Peeves:
Ask for a Recommendation:

Class:
Teacher:
Office Hours:
Phone Number:
Email:
Teacher's Pet Peeves:
Ask for a Recommendation:

Class:
Teacher:
Office Hours:
Phone Number:
Email:
Teacher's Pet Peeves:
Ask for a Recommendation:

Class:
Teacher:
Office Hours:
Phone Number:
Email:
Teacher's Pet Peeves:
Ask for a Recommendation:

Class:
Teacher:
Office Hours:
Phone Number:
Email:
Teacher's Pet Peeves:
Ask for a Recommendation:

Class:
Teacher:
Office Hours:
Phone Number:
Email:
Teacher's Pet Peeves:
Ask for a Recommendation:

My Study Buddies

Class:
Study Buddy:
Phone Number: Email:
Birthday:
EVERYBODY IS SOMEBODY SPECIAL (special interests):

Class:
Study Buddy:
Phone Number: Email:
Birthday:
EVERYBODY IS SOMEBODY SPECIAL (special interests):

Class:
Study Buddy:
Phone Number: Email:
Birthday:
EVERYBODY IS SOMEBODY SPECIAL (special interests):

Class:
Study Buddy:
Phone Number: Email:
Birthday:
EVERYBODY IS SOMEBODY SPECIAL (special interests):

Class:
Study Buddy:
Phone Number: Email:
Birthday:
EVERYBODY IS SOMEBODY SPECIAL (special interests):

PHOTON'S
10 Facts of Academic Success

1. 30 Days of Repetition to Develop Great Study Habits

2. School is All About the Facts: Organize Study Materials!

3. Prepare a Comfortable Study Room

4. Daily **SMARTGRADES** Test Review Notes to Ace Tests

5. Writing Is Rewriting (5-25X)

6. Ask for Proofreading Help!

7. Energize: Real Food Energy

8. Energize: Self-Esteem Energy

9. Energize: Sleep Energy (9-11 P.M.)

10. All Teachers Say 4 Things:
    1. Read a Chapter
    2. Write a Paper
    3. Solve a Problem
    4. Ace a Test

EVERYBODY IS SOMEBODY SPECIAL

PHOTON
SUPERHERO OF EDUCATION
www.BooksNotBombs.com

PHOTON
EVERY DAY AN EASY A

Dark Ages Despair.
PHOTON Is Here.

Enlightenment Is Her Destiny.
World Peace Is Her Legacy.

Nurture the Human Brain.
Keep Planet Earth Sane.

Ignorance Is the Enemy.
Education Is the Remedy.

SMARTGRADES
SCHOOL NOTEBOOKS
Will Prevail.
No Student Will Fail.

Students and Educators Are a Tea
Good Grades Become Grand Drea

Ignorance Is Bitter Not Bliss.
I Seal this Promise with a Kiss

BUY NOW!
AMAZON 2 DAY SHIP
GLOBAL BOOKSTORES

EVERY DAY AN EASY A
TOTAL RECALL
YOUR STUDY ROOM IS UNDER NEW MANAGEMENT
SMARTGRADES SCHOOL NOTEBOOKS AND ACADEMIC PLANNER

EVERYBODY IS SOMEBODY SPECIAL
www.BooksNotBombs.com

PHOTON

SUPERHERO of EDUCATION ®

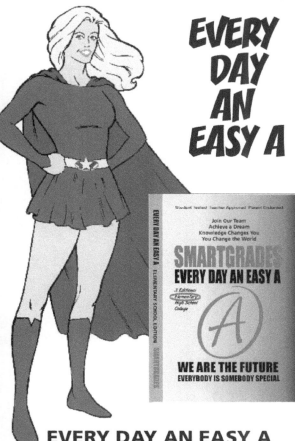

EVERY DAY AN EASY A

EVERY DAY AN EASY A

3 Editions: Elementary, High School, College

ACE EVERY TEST EVERY TIME

All Global Bookstores

www.BooksNotBombs.com

EVERYBODY IS SOMEBODY SPECIAL

---

1 Minute Time Management Class
10 Steps to Success

Step 1 ☐
Make a Daily Action Plan
Write Down Your Big Goals

Step 2 ☐
Set Your Priorities
Urgent, Important, Low, and Optional

Step 3 ☐
Breakdown Your Dreams
Breakdown Big Goal into Smaller Steps
List Steps Necessary to Complete Big Goal

Step 4 ☐
Divide and Conquer
Take Baby Steps Toward Reaching Goal
Crawl. Walk. Fly. Soar...

Step 5 ☐
Use Time Logs: Estimated Vs. Actual Time
e.g., Estimate Time for Lunch: 1 Hour
Actual Time: 20 Minutes
40 Minutes for Errands: Bank, Post Office, Store

Step 6 ☐
Life Is a Bumpy Road
Make Time for Delays, Detours,
Distractions, and Disappointments
e.g., Copier Runs Out of Toner and Paper

Step 7 ☐
Use Checkboxes to Keep Track of Completed Tasks

Step 8 ☐
Review and Refine Daily Action Plan
Pay Attention to Strengths and Weaknesses

Step 9 ☐
Celebrate Your Success
Celebrate Job Well Done with Daily Reward

Step 10 ☐
EVERY DAY AN EASY A
www.everydayaneasya.com

Lightning Source UK Ltd.
Milton Keynes UK
UKHW030609110123
415109UK00009B/677